THE FORGOTTEN CHRISTMAS SAINT

Saint Anastasia

By Susan Peek

Illustrated by Martina Parnelli

For Annie, with love

If you were to ask everyone you know to make a list of saints who remind them of Christmas, probably most of the lists would look the same. At the top, of course, would be the Blessed Mother, with dear Saint Joseph right below.

After them? Well, you can bet your Christmas stocking that Saint Nicholas would pop up next. After all, he's the true Santa Claus (even if reindeer never pulled him through the sky), and it's impossible to think of Christmas without Jolly old Saint Nick and his bulging sack of toys.

Then would come the Three Kings and the Holy Innocents. Saint Stephen's feast falls the day after Christmas, so he'd probably end up on the lists as well. Saint John the Apostle usually manages to squeeze in, too. And we can't forget Saint Francis, the first one to think of setting up a Nativity Scene. He will always belong to Christmas in a very special way.

Wow, what a wonderful assembly of saints gathered in the Stable!

But . . . hold on a minute! How can this be?

ONE OF THE GREATEST CHRISTMAS SAINTS IS MISSING!

Oh, wait. Whew! Here she comes now – that sweet young girl in the blue cloak with the hood, shyly peeking around the corner. See her? But who is this humble and forgotten Christmas saint who always seems to stay in the shadows?

Let's sneak closer to her and find out . . .

An amazing thing happens when you sneak close and meet Saint Anastasia (for that's the beautiful girl's name). Since she's so near the manger where Baby Jesus sleeps, she has this wonderful habit of taking hold of your hand and gently pulling you closer to Him too. In fact, leading others to the Crib is Saint Anastasia's special job. That's why God has honored her in a way that *no other saint* has ever been honored. God placed her feast on Christmas Day itself! Imagine that! Saint Anastasia is the only saint whose special feast falls on the very day Jesus was born! How much God must love her to give her such a high honor!

But that's not all. Saint Anastasia is also the Patron Saint of Martyrs! The King of Martyrs, born on Christmas Day, chose her for this magnificent glory.

Anastasia's sufferings, like Jesus', started right at birth. Although she wasn't born in a cave like He was, she was baptized in one! Her parents were rich, so she was born in a beautiful mansion. But her father didn't believe in God, and he forbade Anastasia to be baptized. So her mother, along with a trusted servant, had to sneak little Anastasia off to a cave, where a priest baptized her in secret.

Jesus wanted Anastasia to be like Him. That's why she started her life as a child of God in a dark and cold cave, just like He had. But that was only the beginning of the sufferings that would fill Anastasia's life . . .

When she was a child, her mother died. Not only did this leave Anastasia very sad, but it made it harder to practice her faith without her father finding out. She had to sneak to Mass when he wasn't watching. She couldn't visit the Blessed Sacrament as often as she wanted. So guess what she did? She built a little "stable" right inside her heart, where she could talk to Baby Jesus all the time.

Not only did Anastasia have to keep her faith a secret from her father, but she had to hide it from almost everyone else too. You see, all this took place about 300 years after Our Lord was born, and back then it was against the law to love and worship God. If the Roman Emperor (who was like a very powerful king) found out that someone was a Catholic, he would have that person thrown in prison, or even killed. So Anastasia had to be very careful that no one found out she was a Catholic.

But God was taking care of her. One day she met a holy priest named Father Chrysogonus. He taught her how to do everything for the love of Baby Jesus, and he encouraged her to be brave and trust in God when things went wrong. And something was about to go terribly wrong . . .

Her father forced her to marry a pagan!

His name was Publius, and he didn't believe in God. Poor Anastasia! Her wedding was one of the saddest days of her life. She tried to smile and offer it up, but inside her heart was breaking.

At first Publius seemed to love his new wife. He bought her expensive gifts and treated her like a queen. But Publius didn't know Anastasia was a secret Catholic. Whenever he left the house, Anastasia would quickly swap her beautiful dress for ragged old clothes and remove her sparkling jewelry. Disguised as a beggar, she would hurry through the streets of the town with food and medicine concealed in the folds of her cloak. She would sneak into the prison, which was filled with Catholics who had been discovered and arrested. The prison was dark and filthy and scary. The Catholics there were starving and ill-treated by the guards. Some were very sick. Many were afraid, too, because they knew they would be killed unless they gave up their faith. So Anastasia would give them food, then comfort them, doing everything she could to help them be brave.

As time went on, it became harder for her to hide her daily prison visits from her husband. Publius started to suspect something. So one day he hid in the house when she thought he was gone. He watched her trade her normal clothes for rags and head out the door. Curious, he followed in the shadows to see where she went.

When he realized his wife was visiting Catholic prisoners, he was enraged!

Publius dragged Anastasia out of the prison and back home. Furious with her, he demanded to know if she was a Catholic. When she said *yes*, he flew into a rage and grabbed a stick to beat her. He hit her again and again until bruises and cuts covered her body, then he threw her into a room and slammed the door shut. She heard him lock it from the other side, then he stormed out of the house.

Poor Anastasia. She was bleeding and hurt. And very afraid. What would Publius do now that he knew for sure his wife was a Catholic? She felt so alone. She huddled on the floor and tried not to cry.

Suddenly she remembered the little stable she'd built in her heart. How could she have forgotten? She instantly knelt down, shaking and in pain, and imagined she was at the manger with Our Lady and Saint Joseph, holding Baby Jesus in her Only it wasn't pretend, because whenever we talk to Jesus, He truly is there. But Anastasia couldn't see Him, just like we can't see Him when we pray. Nonetheless, He was listening, and it made Him smile when shc hugged Him in her heart and told Him she loved Him and was happy to suffer for Him.

After a few days, Publius left on a trip to faraway Persia. He would be gone for many months. At first Anastasia was excited, because that meant she could start visiting the prison again as soon as her husband was out of the way.

But she was wrong. Publius had ordered his servants to keep her locked inside the house until he returned! Anastasia couldn't believe her ears. Months without Mass! Months without bringing food and medicine to the prisoners! She was beside herself with grief.

To keep up her courage during the long and lonely days, she started writing letters to the holy priest from her childhood, Father Chrysogonus. What was her surprise when he wrote back, telling her that God had shown him a vision of Publius drowning on his journey to Persia!

Sure enough, soon Anastasia received word that the boat her husband had been on was shipwrecked, and Publius died by drowning in the sea.

She prayed for his soul, begged God to have mercy on him, then sold everything she owned. She gave all the money to the poor, and, with a joyful heart, headed straight back to the prison.

When she arrived at the prison, there was a wonderful gift waiting for her. It was a brand new friend! Her name was Theodota, and she visited the Catholic prisoners every day too. Theodota's husband had also died, leaving her alone with three sons. Her oldest son, Evortius, was thirteen, and the other two were about eight and ten. Anastasia and Theodota became instant friends. They traveled the countryside together, visiting prisons and teaching people in secret about Christ. Many were baptized because of them.

As time went on, God gave Anastasia the power to work miracles. She healed so many sicknesses, especially those caused by poison, that soon everyone was calling her "The Deliverer of Potions." The nickname stuck, and even today she is given that title in certain countries. (So if you ever get food-poisoning, she's the one to pray to!)

Then one day, something terrible happened. Anastasia heard that Father Chrysogonus had been arrested! Hc would be put to death!

Anastasia hurried to the prison where Father Chrysogonus was being held. But when she sneaked inside, she was shocked to find the entire prison empty! Where was everyone? What had happened?

She went back outside and asked a person on the street what had happened. He told her the Emperor (who was a very wicked man named Diocletian) had ordered all the Catholics to be killed in one night. Every single one in the prison had been martyred, including her dear friend Father Chrysogonus. Although Anastasia rejoiced that they were now all saints in Heaven, she was still heartbroken that she hadn't been able to say good-bye. She sat down on the sidewalk outside the prison and started to cry.

Some passing soldiers spotted her and came over. "Why are you weeping?" one of them asked.

Between her tears, Anastasia answered, "Because I have lost my friends, who have been cruelly put to death."

By her answer, the soldiers realized she must be a Catholic! Before Anastasia knew what was happening, they arrested her!

Poor Anastasia! Her hands were tied with strong ropes, and she was taken to another prison far away. Even though she had spent so much time visiting prisons, it had always been on the outside of the bars. Now she found herself locked in a cold, damp, and dark cell. How frightened she was!

Once again, she remembered the stable in her heart. She decided to visit it often. She talked to Baby Jesus as much as she could, telling Him her fears and begging Him to make her strong and brave.

An evil soldier named Upian came to tell her that she had three days to give up her Catholic faith, or the Emperor would have her killed. Anastasia replied that three days was too long, as she would never, ever stop loving God! Upian then tried to touch her. Horrified, she begged Jesus not to let the wicked man put a single filthy hand on her. God immediately heard her prayer.

Upian was struck blind on the spot. Instantly his head hurt so much he went wild with pain. He screamed in agony from the headache and ran out of Anastasia's cell in panic.

The other guards were so scared of the power of Anastasia's God that they moved her to a different prison in another town.

Meanwhile, Theodota and her three sons were also discovered to be Catholics and were arrested too! Like Anastasia, they were given the choice to either stop loving God or be put to death. Theodota and her children must have been scared, especially when they saw what the soldiers would do to kill them. If they didn't give up being Catholics, they would be burned to death. But they knew God would give them the grace to be brave. God never lets us down!

Theodota's oldest son, Evortius, was the first to be martyred. He was so happy to die for Christ that he went to his death with a big smile on his face. His courage and example helped his two little brothers to accept their deaths too, and Theodota watched as her three children won the glorious Crown of Martyrdom! No mother could be prouder of her sons! With joy she followed them, and within minutes, all four of them were in Heaven, being welcomed with hugs and joy by all the martyrs who had gone before them.

Theodota and her sons are all saints of the Catholic Church. You can pray to them for courage when you're scared. They will be so excited to help you!

Of course Anastasia had no idea what had just happened to her friend. She thought Theodota was still alive and continuing to visit prisoners in another town. She was half-wrong and half-right. Because even though Theodota wasn't alive anymore, she asked God permission to visit one last prisoner before she attended her Welcome Party in Heaven. The other saints up there would just have to wait a few minutes before cutting her cake.

Can you guess which prisoner Saint Theodota came back to earth to see? You guessed it! Saint Anastasia, of course!

Anastasia was in her cold and spooky cell and feeling very, very hungry. The soldiers decided to starve her to death, so they hadn't given her any food. She was trying to talk to Baby Jesus, as she always tried to do, but this time she was so weak and tired that she hardly had the strength to even pray.

Then all of a sudden, the cell lit up with a Heavenly light, and right there in front of her was her dear friend Theodota! Anastasia jumped up to give her a hug, but . . . Theodota had no body! While Anastasia's eyes went all big, Theodota explained to her that she was already dead and in Heaven, so all she had for now was her soul, which is why they couldn't hug each other. But Theodota promised to help her, and told her to be very brave.

Theodota came for sixty nights in a row to visit Anastasia. Each time she left, Anastasia longed for the day that she, too, could go to Heaven with her friend.

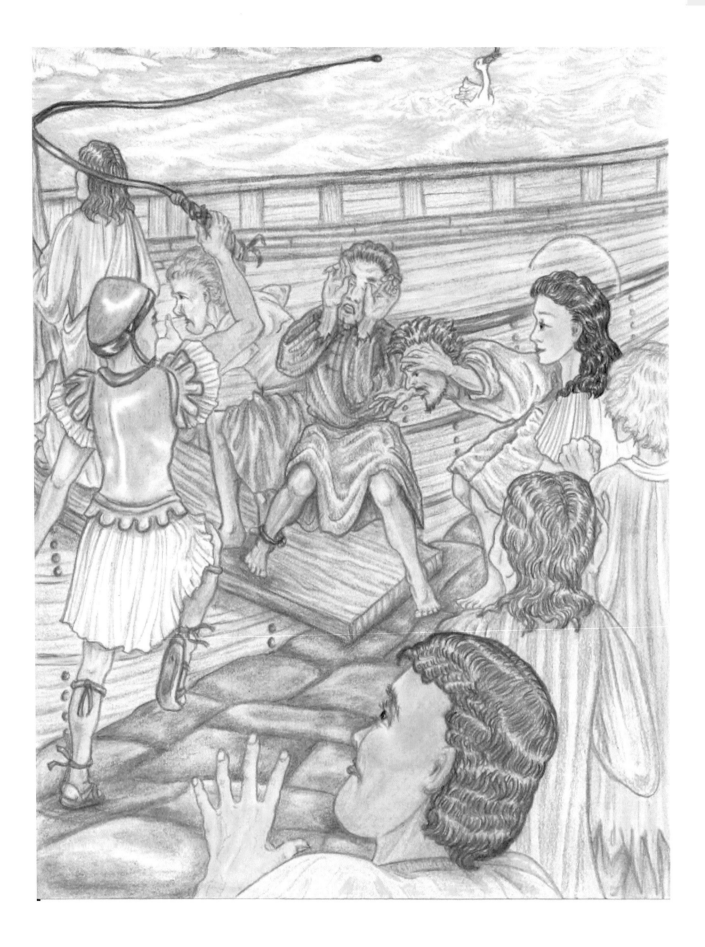

After sixty days, Anastasia was very hungry, but still alive. It was a miracle. The soldiers must have realized they couldn't kill her by starving her, so they came and led her out of her cell. She didn't know where they were taking her. They marched her straight out of the prison and all the way to the shore of a nearby river, where a huge boat was docked. She wondered what was going on.

Everywhere around her were other prisoners. Anastasia tried to count them. There were one hundred and twenty! But these prisoners weren't Catholics. They were criminals! All of them had mean faces and beady eyes and Anastasia realized they were thieves and murderers and outlaws. The soldiers herded them all onto the waiting boat, then threw Anastasia aboard as well.

Only one man on the boat looked at her kindly. He came over and told her his name was Eutychianus. He was a Catholic, not a criminal. When she asked him what was going on, he explained to her that hundreds of holes had been drilled into the boat, so that it would fill with water and sink once it reached the middle of the river. That was how the Emperor planned to kill them. Everyone on the boat would drown.

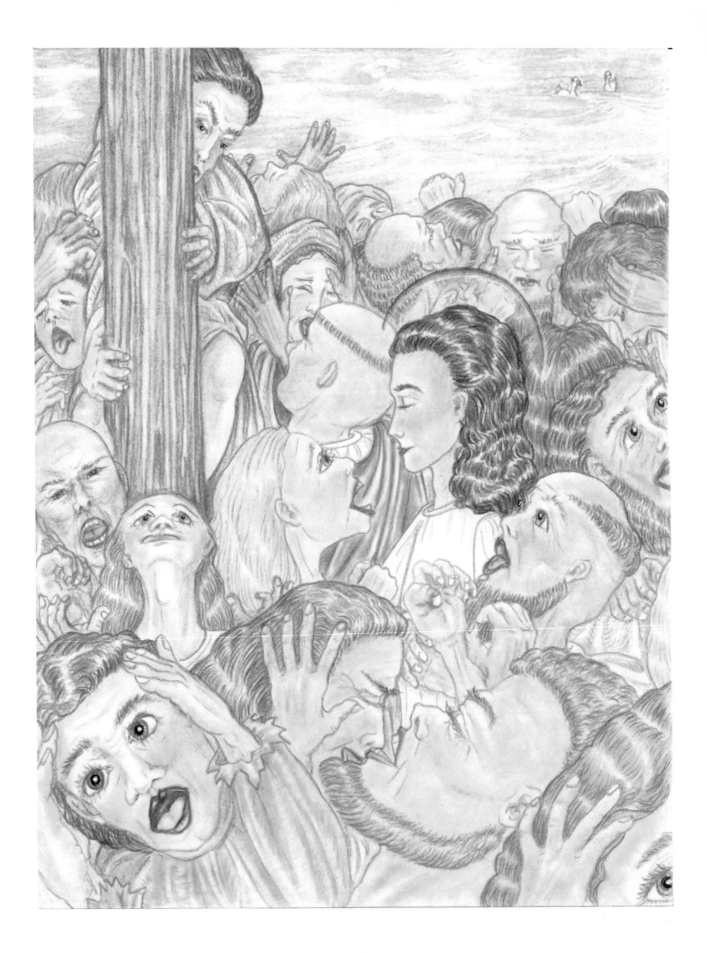

As soon as the soldiers cut the mooring ropes and the boat drifted away from the shore, water began to pour in from all the holes in the sides of the vessel. Within minutes, puddles formed on the floor. More and more water rushed in, until everyone was standing knee-deep in the cold water. The boat started to go down.

As soon as everyone realized the boat was sinking, they panicked. Screaming and crying from all directions filled Anastasia's ears. She and Eutychianus were the only ones who remained calm. Together they started praying. Anastasia asked God not only for courage to face such a horrible death, but also that He would convert all the criminals on board so they wouldn't go to Hell when they died.

All of a sudden, something amazing happened! Saint Theodota appeared in the sky, bathed in glorious, blinding light. She had a huge smile on her face. She gave Anastasia a wink (and probably gave Eutychianus one too), then she took her position at the front of the boat. All one hundred and twenty passengers watched in awe as Saint Theodota, gliding in the air, steered the boat to the other shore. Miraculously, it did not sink! Everyone was safe and alive!

As soon as Saint Theodota disappeared, the criminals were so excited that they surrounded Anastasia and Eutychianus, begging to be baptized. They knew now that the Catholic God was the true God, because only He could work a miracle so great.

So on that day, one hundred and twenty people were baptized and became children of God.

Later on, when Emperor Diocletian found out what had happened, he was furious. He told them he would kill them if they didn't give up their new faith. Every single one of them chose to be martyred, rather than stop being Catholics. So instead of drowning and going to Hell, one hundred and twenty people became saints and martyrs, and all because of Anastasia's prayers.

Now you know why she is the Patron Saint of Martyrs!

But what, you may ask, happened to Anastasia after that? Did she die with the other one hundred and twenty people?

No, she didn't. God had a special martyrdom waiting for her, one that would take a whole lot of courage and an immense amount of love. But Jesus knew Anastasia was up to it. That little stable in her heart wasn't little anymore. It was huge as a giant palace! And Baby Jesus wanted her to die on the most special day of the year . . .

I bet you know which one. You're right! It was Christmas Day itself!

Bravely, Anastasia went to the death that Emperor Diocletian had decided on. She was going to be tied to four pillars with a fire lit beneath her until she died.

Of course Anastasia must have been scared. It would be impossible not to be! But she thought of all her friends in the prisons who had done this before her. Soon she would be with them again. Saint Chrysogonus, Saint Evortius and his two little brothers, Saint Eutychianus . . . and her dear Saint Theodota! All would be waiting for her in Heaven.

So with a huge, brave smile, Anastasia told Baby Jesus she loved Him, and walked towards the waiting flames . . .

After a few moments of pain, it was over. Anastasia opened her eyes and she was at the Heavenly Manger. God the Father had brushed the clouds with red and green to celebrate His Son's birthday. All of Anastasia's friends were gathered in the stable to welcome her, but they stepped aside to give her the special place of honor by Baby Jesus's Crib.

Saint Theodota came forth and tied a red sash around her waist, which only martyrs were allowed to wear. Then Anastasia saw the Blessed Mother approaching. There she stood, the Queen of Heaven, in her Christmas robe and a splendid crown, studded with green emeralds and deep red rubies.

All of Heaven fell silent as Mary gathered Baby Jesus in her arms and handed Him to Anastasia. How happy she was to finally hold Him Whom she had loved and served her whole life.

Jesus smiled and suddenly Anastasia knew she was His Christmas gift too.

And forever she will remain God's Special Christmas Saint.

The End

About the Author

Susan Peek is a wife, mother of eleven children, and a Third Order Franciscan. Her passion is writing novels of obscure saints and heroes, especially for teens. She is an active member of the Catholic Writers' Guild and is currently working on two parallel series: *"God's Forgotten Friends: Lives of Little-known Saints,"* for young adults, and *"God's Forgotten Friends for Children,"* of which this book is the third. Her other books for children include *Animals of God, Volumes One and Two,* also illustrated by Martina Parnelli, and *Saint Rudolph and the Reindeer*, illustrated by Anne Peek.

You can visit her at www.susanpeekauthor.com.

About the Illustrator

Artist and writer Martina Parnelli resides in western Michigan where she enjoys learning about the local flora and teaching the chickadees to eat from her hand. She takes an interest in matters historical and medicinal, as well as all things relating to home craft. As an author, she has written numerous poems, some stories and several plays. She also enjoys composing music. Her books for children include *"Fat John, His Little Lamb, and the Two Wise Owls"* co-authored with M. Roberto Angelorum and published by Leonine Publishers. Her delightful *Little Runty* series tells the accounts of the Holy Family with the donkey that was with them at Bethlehem. And her adult/ teens books *Who Shall Wear the Wedding Veil?* and *Love's Labour Started* are available as well through her website: www.martinaparnelliauthor.co

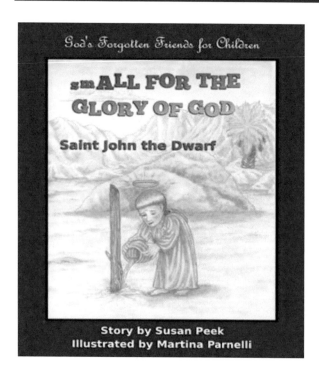
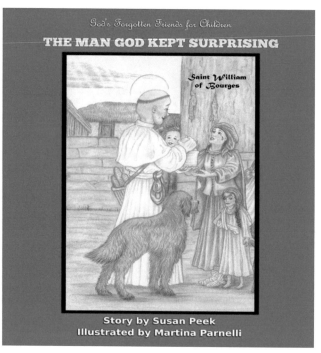

Did you know that reviews sell books?

If you have enjoyed this story, or other books by Susan Peek or Martina Parnelli,

please consider posting a brief review on Amazon, Goodreads, or your favorite book site.

Even a sentence or two would make the authors so happy!

Thank you and God bless!

Made in United States
Troutdale, OR
11/21/2023

14817996R00026